How I Got Over
Stories of Faith & Courage in the Face of Adversity

How I Got Over
Stories of Faith & Courage in the Face of Adversity

Tamatha A. Davis
With Co-Authors:
LaTroy Broadnax · Lakesha Davis
Elena Leno · Scotti Taylor

Preface

The longer I live, the more people I meet that have experienced extreme difficulties and issues in their lives. Until recently, I would just sit in horror as they shared their stories wondering how they made it through. Recently, I became one of them. I lost my right leg above the knee due to a rare vascular disorder. As I endured my very own trial, I began to write about it. I began to document my journey because I now know how people are able to make it through, how they are able to get over the difficulties and adversities they face. In this book we share those stories. Stories that will cause you to sit in horror as they share, but instead of allowing you to wonder we actually share how we made it over.

It was important to write a book like this because so many of us face these types of problems and no one ever tells us how to survive them. In this book we attempt to do just that from each author's unique perspective using their unique story.

This is actually my second anthology. My first – ***Joyous Journey of Loss: Finding Joy in the Midst of Difficult Circumstances*** is similar. However, it is more about loss. This book focuses on the difficulties we face and how to overcome them. My first book was a devotional book entitled *40 Days to Freedom: A Woman's Daily Devotional*. I have also written a 'how to' book – *Self-Publishing in 7 Easy Steps* and published several books under the publishing company that I own – Sivad Publishing.

"No, in all these things we are more than conquerors through him who loved us."
Romans 8:37

Table of Contents

Poems by t.a. davis

Drowning
A Poem of Praise to God

Many of us with stories like this often feel like we are drowning...

Drowning

Into the sea

Dive in

Wade in the water

Loose yourself in the waves

They come up high

And overtake you

You are suffocating

You can't breathe

Reach up for help

He grabs your hand

Leads you gently to shore

You are safe again

Whole

Happy

Free

A Poem of Praise to God

For in your shelter, you will
HIDE *me.*
Under your mighty my wings you will
PROTECT *me.*
By your strong arms you will
UPHOLD *me.*

*You are my **God ETERNALLY**.*
*I am your **daughter**-beloved **FOREVER**.*

*Thank you for your great **LOVE** that*
ENCOMPASSES *me.*
*Thank you for your **FAVOR** that*
SURROUNDS *me.*
*Thank you for your **MERCY** that*
FORGIVES *me.*

*You are my **God FAITHFULLY**.*
*I am your **daughter** beloved **EVER MORE**.*

*Thank you for your **WORD** that*
*gives me **HOPE**.*
*Thank you for your **PRESENCE** that*
*gives me **PEACE**.*
*Thank you for your **SPIRIT** that*
*gives me **STRENGTH**.*

*You are my **God** who **LOVES** me.*
*You are my **King** who **HELPS** me.*
*You are my **Father** who **PROVIDES** for me.*

*You are my **Lord** who **SUSTAINS** me.*
*You are my **Husband** who **ADORES** me.*
*You are my **Friend** who **CARES** for me.*
*You are my **Savior** who **DIED** for me.*

*I am your **daughter** - beloved who **LIVES** for you!*

Introduction

In this book you will meet five average people just like you – four women and one man, who share their stories. However, they share stories of difficulties they have faced in life. They share about time when they wanted to give up, and when life was just too hard. You have met people like this. Maybe you are one of them.

Where do we go to share our pain and our agony with what life has handed us? How do we overcome the seemingly insurmountable obstacles that some of us face? How can we move beyond the hurt and disappointment with our station in life? In this book you will find out how as each person shares not only their story, but how they overcame it. How they made it to the other side.

In *How I Got Over* you will learn how they faced adversity and survived, so just maybe when and if you ever face a trial such as this you will have the necessary tools to get over as well.

"Who is the one who overcomes the world, but the one who believes that Jesus is the Son of God?" 1 John 5:5

Perfection in the Imperfection
Scotti's Story

Chapter One

Married at 25 to a man I had known since elementary school and pregnant at 26, I had grandiose visions of an absolutely perfect life. I had certainly never planned on being a special needs mom, and never expected anything else than both a perfect birth and a perfectly healthy child. For me, perfection was something I had always pushed for incessantly hard. Growing up in Texas, looks mattered, and being the best at everything was expected and required. I was a pageant kid and a competing dancer. I was a cheerleader and an A student.

When the natural cycles of life caused failure or friction, I had no coping mechanisms and would fall into a downward spiral of self-sabotage as a result. Throughout my young life, as is natural, I fell short of perfection time and time again, and sadly, I did not have the tools in place to enable me to grow my character, push through, and become something better through those many moments. I was caught in a never-ending cycle of trying to look the part and act the part, while inside feeling constantly inadequate. When things fell apart, as they do, I fell apart.

Chapter Two

This is my story to tell. How does it fit in to having a special needs child? I believe that the shame, anxiety, and guilt of my trauma and abuse fed into the early birth of my preemie child. I have been told to be quiet, I have been told to *"not rock the boat"*, I have been told *"I don't see how that could have happened."* What happened to me made my family look not only less than perfect, but actually bad. Consequently, besides my husband, I waited until I was 40 years old to tell anyone else. In typical victim-shaming style, the person I told first said, *"Don't you dare tell anyone." "Don't you dare cause problems for the family."*

Chapter Three

I went into early labor and gave birth to my first daughter, Drew, at 26 weeks gestation. She weighed one pound 12 ounces. At that time, I was enjoying a wonderful career as an art director and graphic designer for a well-known aquarium in California. I had fought long and hard to achieve my position, and after having moved to California alone and having worked several grinding menial graphic design jobs, for the first time in my life I felt secure, stable, and proud of myself. I felt I had achieved my dream career at the dream workplace. I mean, I went scuba diving at lunch and worked with incredibly brilliant flip-flop-clad scientists! After years of struggle, partying, alcohol binging, and the basic nonsense of rebellious youth, I had actually made it personally and professionally by the skin of my teeth without anyone's help but my own. I got married during that time and was blissfully happier and healthier than I had ever been. I had achieved perfection.

Chapter Four

Initially when I got pregnant, I had every intention of going back to work part time after Drew's birth. When I went into early labor and was forced to deliver the baby, it was to date the most traumatic experience of my life. Drew was immediately transferred to a level four NICU where she would remain, having surgery after surgery for the next five months. There were many days we thought she would surely die, and several surgeries we thought she wouldn't make it out of, but she would always fight through, barely hanging on. During those time we clung to God's Word. ***"You will not be afraid of the terror by night, Or of the arrow that flies by day; Of the pestilence that [a]stalks in darkness, Or of the destruction that lays waste at noon. A thousand may fall at your side And ten thousand at your right hand, But it shall not approach you."* Psalm 91:5-7** My husband and I were like two ships passing in the night, as I stayed from early in the morning until shift change at 6pm, after which he would arrive after work and stay until late in the night.

When Drew was finally stable enough to be released at five months old, weighing five pounds, her health needs were so immense. My mental health was in such a poor state after the trauma of her birth that I was thrown into life as a stay-at-home mom, and full-time caretaker to a high needs, medically fragile child. Gone were any ideas of me returning to my dream job. I was a grieving human being, grieving both the perfect birth experience I was sure I'd have, and grieving the joy and elation I should have had in those first few months.

I keep a photo in a box next to my bed of me with this man. I open the box to get my contact drops every morning and every night, and I look at this photo. This was prime-time abuse. I look at this little girl and I remember her confusion in the dark. Not knowing what that was between her legs, trying to see under the covers but not having the intelligence to know that boys and girls were different. I can remember every moment of his long fingernails that for some disgusting reason he did not cut. I remember every family member that told me *"I was his favorite."* Every family member that thought I was spoiled rotten because I would throw fits and hold my breath until I passed out. I was left in bed with him, day after day when my grandmother would get up at the crack of dawn and unknowingly leave me there with him while she started her day.

The early years of life with Drew are a blur of doctor appointment after doctor appointment and bouncing from specialist to specialist. Aside from her physical issues, Drew was significantly developmentally delayed, and it was all I could do to keep up with the speech therapists, occupational therapists, and testing. She was labeled with diagnosis after diagnosis. One would be retracted, and two more labels added. Most of the time I pretended like Drew was a completely typical child and ran myself into the ground trying to get her to the level of her neurotypical peers. I dragged my three younger kids around to Drew's gymnastics, dance, music lessons, and Girl Scouts. I taught art in her classroom, I threw lavish birthday parties, and I volunteered for every field trip and every school event. Not only was I trying to create a "normal" life for Drew, but I was also pushing myself forward by sheer will alone, not having allowed myself to address the post-traumatic stress syndrome and depression I really had no idea I was experiencing. I didn't allow myself to grieve the loss of a "normal" pregnancy and birth experience, never sought help, and pushed through trying to find that elusive "perfection." Years later, because of this, I simply tanked.

Chapter Five

Drew is now 19 years old, and I have three younger children. Drew was two years old when I had my second daughter, Reese, who was then only four months old when I became pregnant with my son, Levi. Two years after Levi, even though we thought we were finished, we were blessed with my son Jesse. Yes, I know it sounds crazy! Yes, I was that crazy mom with four kids under six at the playground. As I've already mentioned, those early years are a complete blur, full of appointments and activities. If you saw me on the playground, you might have said I looked like I had it together. Friends would marvel and often say, "*I don't know how you do it*!" If they would have looked a little closer, they would have noticed the frayed edges, and the truth… that most of the time I was hanging on by a minuscule thread. I was a ticking time bomb.

While Drew was certainly significantly developmentally delayed due to her early birth, until around the age of four, her behavior was relatively manageable. At age four, things started to go downhill rapidly. Something would set her off, and her temper tantrums just weren't normal. She would scream for 12 hours straight, beating her head against the wall. If we were in public, she would either throw herself on the ground kicking and screaming, hitting herself in the head, or she would run. With three younger toddlers to worry about, things deteriorated until I couldn't take her out of the house anymore and finding reliable sitters who could handle her needs was often difficult, leaving me more sad and more questioning of my abilities as a mom.

During those early years, we lived on a quiet suburban cul de sac, and everyone knew Drew. They knew to watch for her running down the street, and they knew to ignore the bad behaviors when she would get set off. I frequently had to apologize to our direct neighbors for the noise on the nights where she had screamed all night long, heart-wrenchingly worried that they would call the police or CPS.

I now know enough about health to know that during those years my cortisol levels must have been absolutely through the roof, which definitely wreaked havoc on my adrenals and contributed to significant health issues I've experienced in my current peri-menopausal state. My brain was fried and, I self-medicated with alcohol, and was a heavy subscriber to the *"Mommy Wine Culture."* My rule back then was to just get through until 4:00 p.m., after which I would crack open a bottle of wine and sip through dinner, bath, and bedtime. I often went to sleep wasted and woke up hungover. The alcohol kept me from ruminating on my problems, but I created a monster that I would pay for years later when I learned I could not function without it.

I am approaching fifty years old. Almost everything bad that has happened in my life can be linked back to mental trauma due to this man. A man who I've watched be revered, idolized, and worshipped my entire life. A *"great man,"* a *"cowboy,"* even *"a ladies' man."* The fact that he ran around on my grandmother was overlooked and accepted.

Chapter Six

My cycle was predictable: Drew would have a really bad spell, and subsequently night after sleepless night I would desperately spend all hours on the computer researching medications, supplements, specialists, syndromes, and psychiatrists. The next morning, I would rush to the health food store and drop $300 on supplements, which never worked. At one point, I was actually cooking and dehydrating cows' brains, which I would pulverize into a powder, encapsulate, and feed to her, trying to get her the exact combination of miraculous amino acids. As a vegetarian, this was SO difficult, and the smell was so terrible that my husband couldn't stand to be in the house! I was trying so incredibly hard to "fix" Drew, all the while trying to give the other kids some semblance of a normal life. On top of that, my husband's job required him to frequently travel, often for weeks on end. I'll never forget the absolute, heart-stopping despair I would feel every time he told me he had to travel. I was frightened and felt utterly alone. Often in those early years, I would pack up the kids and travel to Texas, to spend the long weeks with my parents, the minute he left for a trip. As the kids got older and became school aged, that obviously became harder and harder to do.

Once Drew entered Kindergarten, there was the added pressure of trying desperately to keep her at-level, manage her IEP, and with what diagnosis she was being given (everything from ADHD, to Asperger's, to Autism, to bipolar disorder, to Oppositional Defiant Disorder, to Sensory Processing Disorder, to name just a few). Many parents are afraid of labels, but most people don't understand that the diagnoses are the deciding factor in the amount and kind of services your family is provided with. That's why the first thing I tell all families I work with is, *"Do not be afraid of a diagnosis. Get as many as you can, because the more labels you have, the more help you will receive"* These families are usually just like me— grieving the loss of what they thought life would be like for their child and processing the fact that their child is different from their peers. Along with this, there is the excruciatingly slow process of acceptance that these children will most likely face challenges for the rest of their lives.

He bred evil in me. He bred confusion. He bred shame. Guilt. Disgust for myself. Hate. I watched him die and was expected to cry at his funeral. I watch others tiptoe around me now to keep me quiet, scared that I would tarnish the family's reputation. I am quieted, I am still shamed, I am admonished for *"causing problems in the family."* I consistently protect others. I constantly am thinking of how others would feel. I never told anyone because I didn't want to hurt anyone, cause problems for others.

Chapter Seven

As Drew bounced around from elementary school to elementary school while I tried to find the perfect class, the perfect teachers, and the perfect setting for her, I grew more and more attuned to the workings of the public school system. Becoming a special needs advocate for families needing help navigating the very difficult education and state systems was not in my playbook, but over the last 19 years, I have had to fight so hard on so many issues pertaining to Drew's health, education, and services provided by the state, that I know the system inside and out. The more people I met and collaborated with including Him, the more questions I knew to ask. The bible says, ***"Call to me and I will answer you and tell you great and unsearchable things you do not know."*** **Jeremiah 33:3**

And the more rights I knew I had. Throughout those years navigating the system, I learned that because I was white, privileged, and generally an easy person to get along with, I got more help, as sad as that sounds. I quickly realized that there is no one who will come out and tell you about the myriad services that are offered unless you know exactly what to ask for, so I made it my mission to pass along information to as many families and parents as I could. Soon enough, I found myself walking families through the process over several months and years at a time, and there is no better feeling than when a parent reaches out to me after a two-year-long process and their lives have just opened up. They are no longer as financially strapped, as terrified of the system, as complacent with their schools, and they understand how to hold people accountable when it comes to the education and advancement of their child.

Truly, there is no better feeling in the world! Occasionally there will be hiccups as the children age through the system, and most times those families will give me a call and it's a simple thing I can help with. Also, because of some videos I've shared through social media, I've had the opportunity to guide people from all over the US. I may not always know the answers, but I always know how to find the answers and I take pride in my determination to help. There is truly no better feeling than when a mom, who has been at the end of her rope with a struggling marriage and financial hardship, calls me up and tells me she's got that first check in hand or those respite hours ready. I can hear the relief, in their shaky, happy voices, of finally having the resources to help build a support system for their family. It brings me right back to those hard years every time and my heart soars for their futures.

Chapter Eight

Through Drew's struggles, I have learned so much. She is a fighter. She has fought for every single milestone she has achieved. She is strong-willed and knows exactly what she wants, and she will not take no for an answer. These gifts give me peace when the horrible thoughts creep in of *"what will happen to her when I'm gone?"* She is funny and clever, with the memory of an elephant. I often joke that God gave me Drew because I simply have to call out to her, throughout the week, things that we're out of, and on shopping day, she can rattle everything off without falter.

The most important thing being Drew's mom has taught me is that beauty lies in the eyes of the beholder; one just has to adjust their lenses. Take off your perfect lenses. Put on the ones with the cool filters, the ones that make every scene look colorful and magical. Every day, every month, every year that passes, my own lenses get clearer.

Chapter Nine

I am close to fifty years old. And now I am finally free.

I have been a far from perfect mom, but what I hope I can teach my children is perseverance. ***"And not only this, but [c]we also exult in our tribulations, knowing that tribulation brings about perseverance; and perseverance, proven character; and proven character, hope; and hope does not disappoint, because the love of God has been poured out within our hearts through the Holy Spirit who was given to us"*. Romans 5:3-5** It is a lifelong struggle to attain personal growth, and even when one wall comes down, six more go up. Life is so hard, but we get up. We throw the party. We dress up. We go to all of the places.

THE
TAYLOR
FAMILY

DAUGHTER (DREW), HUSBAND (JEFF) & ME

The Final Goodbye
Lakesha's Story

You taught me everything, but how to live without you. Who would have thought the phone call I received on June 24, 2012, would change my life forever?

The call simply went like this: *"Hello, hey you need to get to granny's house right now; we don't know how much longer she will live."*

I knew in my heart I was not ready to say goodbye to my granny. All I could do was drop the phone and rush out the door. Now, any other day it seems like her house was right around the corner, but this day I don't know why it felt like she lived out of town. My thoughts were racing, and the tears were flowing. I was nervous.

I started praying, *"Please let me make it to see my Queen one last time."*

Finally there, I jumped out the car and ran through the door screaming, *"Where is she!"*

As I rushed inside her bedroom, I noticed her just lying there. She had already started shallow breathing. I walked up to her and started rubbing my hand through her soft gray hair. The tears were running down like a waterfall.

I kissed her forehead and said, *"Granny I'm here. It's me, Keeshee. I'm here granny, please don't go."*

She looked at me with one tear falling from the side of her left eye, as if she wanted me to know that she would be with me forever. She was tired, and I know she was, but I was being selfish, and didn't want to let her go.

Time started passing by and she began to get colder and colder. My momma knew I needed a break from crying, so she asked me to come ride with her.

I looked over at my granny and said, *" Don't you go anywhere. I'll be right back."*

No longer than 30 minutes after we left, the call came. I felt my soul leave my body, a gust of wind hit my face, as if I'm falling off a cliff with nothing to hold on to.

"She's gone," I yelled!

Here I am about to bury the only person who ever loved me.

I screamed at God, *"Bring my granny back right now, or you are going to have to take me. I hate you!"*

I started believing there wasn't any God.

*"Why my granny? "*I screamed! I thought grannies were supposed to live forever!

I stopped praying, I stopped going to church. I hated God; I hated myself. I sat there day after day trying to figure out how and what I could do to die and go be with my granny. For months I questioned that man everyone called God; I cried over and over, trying to understand.

From that day forward, I felt my life shift in a different direction. I began shutting down. I locked myself in my room. I started neglecting my kids, going through a divorce, losing my mind and myself. I was so sad that I couldn't move. The only person to ever show me pure love, who had prayed for me, and the only one I trusted, was gone. I have never lost someone that close to me. I didn't know what to do. I had to find some way to not feel the pain. I had to find a way to die.

Then the phone rings. It's an old friend I met when I was 14. We get to talking and I'm explaining to him what was going on and that I wasn't in a good place in my life right now. He suggested coming over so we could catch up. I wasn't really up to having any company, but oh well why not. He comes over and we start talking. Then he pulls out a bag with white powder in it.

I started asking him, "*Wait, why are you putting that up your nose?*"

Heck I didn't know what it **was**. I never used drugs. So, at the time, I'm confused. Not knowing what I was about to get myself into, I asked him if I could try it. As he handed me the bag, he made sure to let me know that it was one of the best batches of cocaine he had in a while. I asked him if this would make me feel better. Shaking his head, yes, I looked down, grabbed the straw, and snorted the biggest line on the plate. My eyes rolled and my head fell back. I felt something. I also thought I heard the door slam, and something hit the ground. Yeah, something hit the ground all right. It was me! This was the beginning of my downfall and not my death.

That's right, one line turned into a whole 8 ball. I started snorting cocaine every day, nothing less than a hundred dollars per day. I started liking it so much that I sold everything I could to buy it. I soon moved in with a guy who had just lost his wife. His name was Jackpot, and I used him. I waited for him to leave one day, hurried, and called my dealer, and sold everything in his house for a hundred-dollars' worth of drugs.

Next thing I know I'm on the streets and I have graduated to heroin, speed, sherm, and anything that would get me high. I even had several out of body experiences. One day I called the funeral home and told them to send a hearse. When they inquired about who had died, I told them it was me. After all these different drugs, it left me wondering why I was still alive?

One day my best friend decided he wanted to go over to his aunt's house. They introduced me to what I thought would surely take me out.

Auntie grabbed the pipe and said, "Pull *slowly, imma get you high today.*"

I remember pulling on the pipe thinking *ok here come those bells everyone was talking about.* Crack cocaine had become my new best friend. For eight years it tore me from God, my kids, and my family. I had hit the bottom, I lost everything. Most importantly I lost myself. I didn't care anymore. There was no stopping me from going where my Queen was. I was hooked, spending paychecks, income tax, heck I was even stealing out of stores. My daughter Bri had to now take on the responsibility of a mother because I was too busy getting high. I made my child go out and beg for money so she could feed her brother and little sister. I even screamed at her when she didn't come back with a cigarette. One time I snatched her purse and stole her money.

Then, when I got broke, I would run to my mother and tell her to give me money or I was going to run in front of a bus, or have the dealer come and kill her if she didn't give me money. *Why didn't I just take a gun and shoot myself in the head?* But I couldn't because I knew better! All I did was torture my family.

My actions had caused me to neglect what was important. My kids did not deserve to lose their mother to depression and drugs. CPS was called on me but using my kids pee, I always passed.

I kept fighting with God asking him, "*Is this what you* want?

I smoked $3,000 in a week. I was smoking back-to-back nonstop for days. During that time, I started realizing the people I was getting high with didn't love nor care about me. They **were** using me to buy drugs. Plus, the high wasn't good anymore.

Then one day I met a stranger who walked up to me and said, "*Why are you doing this to yourself?*"

I explained to him that I have nothing to live for and I want to die and go be with my granny.

He then said, " *I can see you are a child of God, and you will never see her again until you get yourself together. She is not happy with you right now, and she doesn't want to see you.*"

Before I could get mad and say something, he cut me off quickly by saying, "*You are too beautiful to be trying to kill yourself!!*"

I couldn't believe he could see my heart through all the drugs I was doing. It was then I felt something reach down and touch my face with an incredibly soft touch. The stranger had disappeared. While I was looking around for him, my phone rang.

It was another frantic caller on the other end. "*Kesha, he's gone!*"

My anxiety goes up and I ask, "*Who's gone?*"

I did not know that the caller would then tell me that my best friend, the person who I first started getting high with was now dead. Now I started thinking. Had I not stopped to talk to that stranger I would have been with him getting high, and that would be somebody calling my family to tell them I was dead. God saved me! I knew then that God didn't want me to die.

I started searching for help trying to save me from myself. So, I got down on my knees and I prayed, and I cried and cried and prayed some more. I asked God to please take all the pain and hurt away. I asked Him to take the addiction away. While I was praying, a song was playing in the background. It was saying to *let go and let God have His way*. Confirmation: that's what that was. I started fighting that demon that came and stole my peace of mind.

I called this rehab, and a guy answered the phone. I said, *"Sir, I don't know you, and you don't know me. I have no money, but if I stay out here any longer, I'm going to die.*

Tony Springer said, *"What's your address? You stay right there and I'm sending someone now. "*

I remember looking up at the sky, while sitting outside the door of the house waiting for my ride saying, *"Thank you God for sending your angel."*

As a matter of fact, through my recovery, God sent me a couple of angels: Tony Torres, Troy Seals, and Tony West. Each of them played a huge role in my recovery. Just when I thought I was on a road to recovery from drugs and my relationship with my mother, my faith and my recovery was about to be tested.

My mom had become extremely sick, and this time she would not be recovering like everyone thought she would. My mother and I were never close. But I would run to her every beckoning call no matter what time or day it was. Momma had hurt me so much throughout my life. She talked like a dog behind my back.

She let men molest me, and when I told her she would say, *"Oh you like it, so get out my face"*.

All I ever wanted was her to love me like a mother was supposed to love her child. Because my sister and I did not have the same dad, Momma said I was a mistake. That will sit on my heart forever, but that would not stop me from being next to my mother the last week of her life. I sat there for a week begging her to open her eyes so that we could have one last conversation.

She shocked me and opened her eyes only to say, "*I'm about to die*".

I sat in that hospital room all day and night, crying, praying, singing, and just wishing momma would open her eyes and just say she loved me. I sat there by myself, thinking God had given momma and me these last few days together alone to make things right between us.

I screamed at her saying, "*Momma, you are leaving me so damaged, and you won't even open your eyes and say you are sorry. You are the reason I started using drugs, you hated me. I was your oldest and you treated me like I wasn't even your child. You called me a crackhead. You said I was a whore just like my daddy. You tore me and my sister apart. You made us hate each other, and you didn't fix it. You made me lose my kids and you were giving me money to buy dope.*"

But momma wouldn't open her eyes, and the few times she did, she wouldn't look at me.

"Oh, now you are ashamed," I said. *"You thought it would be your other child standing beside your bed, but no, it's the one you hated! Yea, your mistake child! The one you thought would be somewhere smoking instead of by her mother's side. Your favorite baby girl is on a cruise while you lay here dying."*

As the days passed, I felt something in me was about to be released. I just felt weird. I was crying so much it was like pressure being released from my body, my mind, and my soul.

"*God is that you?*" See, I had been fighting with God for eight years, so, as I looked up in the sky, I heard God say, "*It's time for you to forgive your mother.*"

God knows that I love my mother. Despite all the hurt she put me through, I was able to forgive her. Before momma passed away. I whispered in her ear, "*Momma you don't have to worry about me picking that pipe up again, I'm done. You can rest now. I forgive you and I love you. Too bad you didn't love me."*

The time came for me to say goodbye to my mother. Right after I whispered that in her ear, momma went on home to be with the Lord. On October 6, 2019, I officially made no more relapses. No more drugs! Who knew that my mother's passing would be the beginning to the peace I have been looking for forever? That release I felt was God taking away every hurtful thing my mother ever did or said to me. He was assuring me that I would be at peace and that He would never leave me nor forsake me. **"for the Lord your God goes with you; he will never leave you nor forsake you."** **Deuteronomy 31:6b**

After we buried momma, I got back to my Bible. I started praying daily, sometimes all day. I started begging God to forgive me. I stopped smoking and I started reading my *Daily Encounters with God*. I'm at peace now. I love God. He has forgiven me and has given me a new drug-free life. Once again, God saved a lil ole' wretch like me. And the cold part is, I don't deserve it. I have my kids back in my life and six grandbabies to keep me going. Depression is real, and addiction is a fight. You have to take one day at a time, but with God on your side all things are possible. ***"Jesus looked at them and said, "With man this is impossible, but with God all things are possible"*** **Matthew 19:26.** I'm so happy my relationship with God is back, and that He forgave me, and He never left my side. **1 John 1:9** says, **``*If we confess our sins, He is faithful and righteous to forgive us our sins and to cleanse us from all unrighteousness.*"**

All I had to do was ask. See, granny told me God was not done with me yet, and finally, I have my life back. October 6, 2021, made two years that I have been drug free! I am saddened that I had to say goodbye to my granny and my mother but elated that I have said the final goodbye to drugs!

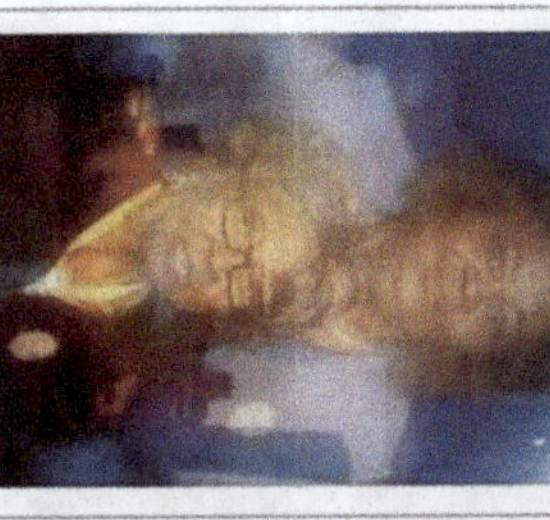

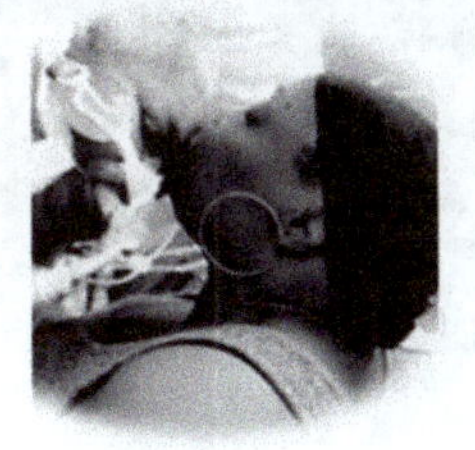

Granny (Hazel decd.), Momma (Constance decd.) & Me

Children (Ambrisha, Westley & Kaneisha)

Grandchildren

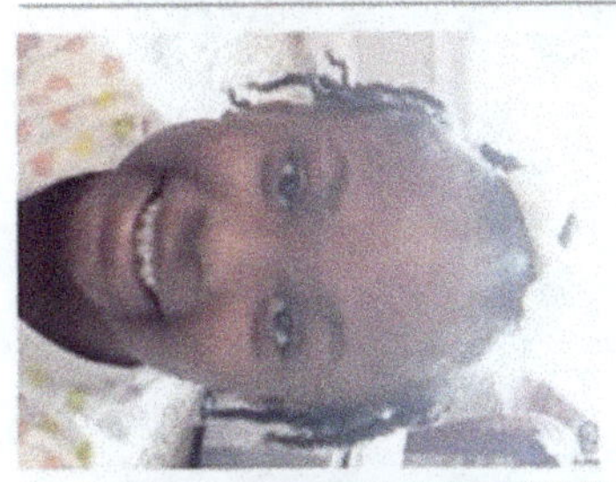

Deliverance is Mine
LaTroy's Story

My grandfather died holding my hand in 1995. Without a male role model growing up, in my early 20s I began to make bad choices in my life. I needed deliverance from these bad choices. I'll share what I mean by that. On a typical day I got home to my mom's house, and she started to fuss at me. I was trying to tell her about a song that I wrote called *Hold Your Head Up and Keep on Striving*. I am a singer and a songwriter. She had made pork chops, which I love, and I had good news! I thought this would be a good evening until she started to go off on me.

She said, *"Troy you're living a dream!"*

When she said that, I was appalled. After that I didn't even want to eat the pork chops because I was so hurt. When she told me that, her words hurt me.

I went into my room and was brought to my knees. I said, *"Lord help me make it."*

By this time, I had started abusing drugs and alcohol. The things she said to me caused me to be in a really bad state of mind. I cried out to God, asking Him to please deliver me.

After that altercation with my mom, I decided that I was going to move to Austin, Texas, and try to live a different life. I had several cousins in Austin, so I decided to go and stay with a friend. Unfortunately, I began to go on the streets and hustle on 12th Street in Austin. These guys knew my cousins. I didn't know any of them, but they helped me. They allowed me to move drugs on 12th Street. Now the guys that they were raised with didn't allow them to do that. So, I was in Austin, and I was hustling to make a living. God had just delivered me from doing primos when I lived in Houston. (Primos are when you add powder cocaine to the marijuana joint).

Sadly, when I got to Austin, the next thing Satan brought to me was cocaine. My cousin had a lot of it, and he was rolling pretty tough. I found myself coming home from work running in to smoke because my cousin and his crew were doing what I used to do. I found myself doing cocaine and indulging in different parties. I knew

God had delivered me from that, so I would pray every time that I would smell it and walk to my room. God brought me through that.

I would pray and I would tell Satan, *"When God delivers me from this, what will you bring next, Satan? "*

"Your adversary, the devil, prowls around like a roaring lion, seeking someone to devour." 1 Peter 5:8b Well, this drug demon began to chase me in my sleep and would call me to do cocaine. The lusting demon also comes with this drug. The devil would try to make me want to be with a lady. I would pray to God to give me strength. This demon would have me looking for dates. I would hate to do this drug because it would have me up all night. I also didn't like the fact that it made my nose hurt.

I would pray to God, *"God please deliver me from this!"*

I also did marijuana and drank alcohol. The moment I started drinking is when the demon would attack me. I kept believing that God would bring me my deliverance. I found myself staying away from those that wanted to party like that. I found myself praying more. One day God gave me a new song. And the words were:

I tried to go on my own.
I tried to do what's right,
but I change the right.

It's too long and
now I'm coming home.

Jesus I'm sorry the way that seems so right.
Now I'm in the darkness and I cannot see
the light.

I know you have the key
if you would just let me free.

I would do anything but now did they laugh
in my face
and say that you won't plead my case.

I'm holding onto my faith.
I'm trusting you make a way.

I know you'll dry my tears and
deliver me from all fears.

If I would just let you in,
I know that you will defend me.

Jesus I'm sorry the way that seem so right
and now I'm in the darkness and I cannot
see the light.

I love my mom; however, we have not always been close. I cannot say how we made it over from the issues we faced.

One day I asked my grandfather, *"Pawpaw, why does my mom treat me like she does?"*

He told me to sit down so he could tell me. He said, *"Son, it is because you look so much like your daddy."*

This is so cold because my dad beat my mother. I'm still hurt behind this today. My mom and I have a blessed mother and son relationship. However, if I had a father to stay on me, I think I would have made better choices, in my finances for example. I look back at times of being addicted to drugs, the robbing and being shot at. I know how I made it over and I never gave up. I told my pastor that I will never give up on God.

God gave me wisdom. I received my maturity in Austin, Texas, and I thank God for that. When Satan comes to me on a daily basis in the mind, I thank God that I have His Word.

I had to get to know my spiritual man. Thank God that He has truly blessed me. I love the man that He has made me become. It is a growing daily thing. I love the Lord for the people he has allowed to pass through my life. In Austin, I met my brother and his wife, who have become life-long friends.

God has shown me His power. The devil was trying to make me feel that God didn't hear me. I knew that he was a liar, because the Bible tells us that he is the father of lies. **Proverbs 3:5-6 says** ***"Trust in the Lord with all your heart, And do not lean on your own understanding. In all your ways acknowledge Him, And He will make your paths straight."*** He also says in **Proverbs 14:12** ***"There is a way which seems right to a man, But its end is the way of death."*** I would just rely on the scripture. In **Philippians 3:13b** says, ***"forgetting what lies behind and reaching forward to what lies ahead."*** The Bible says in **2 Timothy 3:16** ***that "All Scripture is [a]inspired by God and profitable for teaching, for reproof, for correction, for [b]training in righteousness;".***

God did give me my deliverance. I thank the Lord for sparing my life once again. The devil would try and bring the temptation back to me in the middle of the day. I would hear a whisper in my ear saying, *"You know you want to do a line of cocaine."* But God gave me the strength I needed to resist the temptation.

In those moments, I would cry out to God, *"Oh God you are my God and my Savior!"*

God said that we only needed faith the size of a mustard seed, and we serve such a great God that He knew that our faith would become low sometimes. It was in those times that the devil would try and make me give up on life, but God would wake me up to see a new day.

I would get up and thank the Lord and say, ***"This is the day that the Lord has made; Let us rejoice and be glad in it!"* Psalm 118:24** I had to tell the devil what God says about me. **"No *weapon formed against you shall prosper.* "Isaiah 54:17a (NIV)** in the name of Jesus! I would also tell Satan to get behind me. *"I rebuke you in the name of Jesus."*

He would try to come through people to get to me. I had to realize again, that no weapon formed against me shall prosper in the name of Jesus. I had to do just like David did in **Psalm 141:3-4a** and ask God to *"Set a guard, O Lord, [a]over my mouth; Keep watch over the door of my lips. Do not incline my heart to any evil thing, To practice deeds [a]of wickedness"*.

It is not strong Troy. It is the Holy Ghost power. I learned that *"But if any of you lacks wisdom, let him ask of God, who gives to all generously and [a]without reproach, and it will be given to him,"* according to **James 1:5**. Wisdom is used in so many different ways. You can't allow Satan to trap you. It doesn't matter what your addiction is. I was really tired of doing this evil to my body. I was tired of being tired.

I remember my mom said one day, *"Troy what is that you doing in there?"*

I said,*" It's just weed."*

She said," *That don't smell like no weed."* This is how I made it over.

She said," *Whatever it is, hurry up and come out of there."*

I was crushing another rock.

I said," *Lord, look at me."* I was facing a mirror.

I said," *I can't stop."*

I began to cry to Him, pleading with Him to take the desire to do drugs away from me. It was a day or two later that Jesus gave me my deliverance. I will say you know you can't fool God. I stopped being around dope and dope dealers. I went into the Lord's house and started receiving my blessings.

You have to know **"The spirit is willing, but the flesh is weak." Matthew 26:41b** When you get your deliverance, the flesh is still weak. Please know this is real. You will feel better. You will look better, but your flesh is weak. Here is a warning. Don't go to a place where they are laughing, smoking, and drinking. The demons will jump on you so fast. It will show you how weak your flesh is. Get up! Don't stay in that mess! Get up screaming, *"Jesus!"* Gather your shortcomings and realize what you did to take you back to the devil's playing field. Stay away from the paths to temptation's lane of pain.

I thank God for another day of love and an eye opener. We have been growing in God. We have learned to be obedient in staying faithful to God. I say we because through all of this God blessed me with a beautiful wife, whom I do not deserve. But I have been happily married for almost nine years! I also have one beautiful daughter who is 17 years old. I thank God every day for the new life He has given me in Christ. Victory is ours in Jesus' name. Don't give up on God, and don't give up on your deliverance! ***".... but thanks be to God, who gives us the victory through our Lord Jesus Christ."* 1 Corinthians 15:57**

WIFE (PAULA), MOM (DEBORAH) & ME

DAUGHTER (MAKAYLA)

GRANDMOTHER (FAYE) & ME

The Most Difficult Part

Tamatha's Story

I thought the most difficult part of this journey was losing my leg. In 2018, my right leg was amputated above the knee due to a rare disease. Peripheral Arterial Disease coupled with the autoimmune disease Sjogren's Syndrome created the perfect storm for lack of blood flow to my extremities. After my leg was amputated, I thought the rest would be easy. Boy, was I wrong! The most difficult part of this journey is the recovery. That is the part I am in now, and what I will attempt to share with you. How did I get over my recovery?

It has been over three years since my initial amputation of my right leg, and I am still not walking. I am still in a wheelchair, and I've had an additional six amputations and numerous hospital stays. I have lost count, but if I had to guess, I would say around eight hospital stays. Each time the goal is for me to get better. However, each time it seems as though I am getting worse. As they cut off half of my big toe, then the other half, then half of my second toe, then the remaining toe, then the remaining three toes that are left, then half of my foot, I wonder how I am getting better. As the pain from these amputations becomes so excruciating that I can no longer bear weight on my left side at all, and my husband must pick me up to do anything that I need to do, I wonder how in the world is this me getting better? No, it feels as though it's me getting worse! However, I have to remember that **"No, in all these things we are more than conquerors through him who loved us."** **Romans 8:37 (NIV)**

As a Christian, I have learned it is better not to complain, which is a good thing. Complaining is what kept the children of Israel out of the promised land. **(Numbers 11)** Therefore, when someone asks me how I am doing, my response is simple: *"I am doing good. Just have a little pain in my foot."* And in all honesty, that is true, but there is so much more.

The wheelchair piece, and not being able to walk has been the most difficult to adjust to. Just imagine sitting on the couch wanting a snack then realizing you are unable to complete a task as simple as that for yourself. Now take it a step further and your child wants a snack.

Since I was in a wheelchair, and unable to walk I was unable to get into what I would learn is the most important room in the house -- the bathroom! A bedside potty and diapers were employed. The diapers -- just in case I could not reach the bedside potty in time with my one leg and all. I didn't want any accidents!

Then there is this whole thing with the incontinence. All I will say about it is it's one of the worst things that has ever happened to me. You actually lose control of your bodily functions. You are placed in quite the predicament not knowing what to expect or when to expect it. Having other people clean you and change your diaper as an adult is a very humbling experience. In fact, everything about incontinence humbling. I have never been this humbled.

I ended up needing six additional amputations after my initial one. My final amputation was half of my left foot. Prior to that I could move around pretty well — bed to chair — chair the couch — chair to potty, and vice-versa. Well, that all ended when my left foot began the healing process, and I could no longer put any weight on it. It got so bad that I would just lay in my bed with pain all over my body and unable to move for fear that something else would be thrown into pain.

I struggled in every way possible of course physically, but emotionally and relationally as well. Many of the relationships closest to me begin to break down. I hated needing others and often denied myself survival level necessities just so I did not have to ask for help. This made those around me especially my husband upset with me because all he wanted was just to serve me, meet my needs to make sure I was happy, comfortable, and well taken care of. Sadly, I punished myself and would not allow him that joy during this time.

I now understand that when they amputated my leg, he felt helpless. The guy known for his problem-solving abilities could do nothing to make blood flow to my leg so that I did not lose it. After I went home and there were actually things that he could help me with, I denied him that as well.

During my recovery, I often thought about David. God allowed him to go so low before he came and delivered and redeemed him. I would think, Lord how much lower! I knew my deliverance was up to God and not me. I would spend hours wondering if I had made one or two different choices, how would my situation have turned out differently? I eagerly expected God to do a miracle and I never lost hope in our God, His faithfulness, His power, and His promises. All I brought to the table and all I had to offer was my faith, and that was enough. *" For God has not given us a spirit of fear, but of power and of love and of a sound mind."* **2 Timothy 1:7 (NKJV)**

Due to the wounds on my left foot that have not healed from amputations, I live in constant pain. Sometimes I think if I could just get the pain to go away, I would be okay. But I know that is not true. I want to walk again, and I will walk again. I am determined! I am a fighter! I will not give up!

One of my favorite verses really in life has become magnified during this time. I have lived on it. It is my meat- my sustenance **Philippians 4:6-7** *" Be anxious for nothing, but in everything by prayer and supplication with thanksgiving let your requests be made known to God. And the peace of God, which surpasses all [a]comprehension, will guard your hearts* *and your minds in Christ Jesus"* So, I will have to say my first step to how I got over in my journey of recovery would simply be to **pray about everything**. There is nothing on this planet or in this universe for that matter visible or invisible that we cannot pray about. The Bible encourages us to" ***Pray without ceasing.*** **" 1 Thessalonians 5:17** We are clearly instructed to pray all the time about everything. In those prayers God desires that we are not anxious, but instead thankful to Him that the answer to our prayer is quickly on its way!

The second step to overcoming my recovery would simply be to **worship God**. There are an estimated 72 times that worship is mentioned in the bible. This is an important aspect to our walk with Christ. We are commanded to worship God. It is one of the reasons for which we were created. He desires our worship. And it is our responsibility to give it to Him freely. Further, worship defeats the enemy according to **2 Chronicles 20:22 *"When they began singing and praising, the Lord set ambushes against the sons of Ammon, Moab, and Mount Seir, who had come against Judah; so, they were [a]routed."***

However, worship does more than just that. It does many things. Worship______:

......*takes our minds off the things of the* **W***orld.*

......*invites God's spirit into* **O***ur situations.*

.... *destroys P***R***ide.*

.... *defeat***S** *the enemy.*

.... *changes the atmosp***H***ere.*

.... *Is an effective sp***I***ritual weapon.*

.......*is an outward ex***P***ression of our love for* *God.*

God enjoys our worship! Oxford dictionary defines worship as *"an expression of reverence and adoration."* As all the beautiful ideas about worship became crystal clear to me, I realized that worship had to be a part of my daily life. I endeavored to worship as much as I could and as often as I could.

The last step in my pursuit to overcome in my recovery process is to **read God's Word**. You know God's Word is extremely powerful. **Hebrews 4:12** says, *"For the word of God is living and powerful, and sharper than any two-edged sword, piercing even to the division of soul and spirit, and of joints and marrow, and is a discerner of the thoughts and intents of the heart."* **(NKJV)** I have learned that whatever you put into your mind is what you will get out. It is how you will live and function. Because of this part of the Christian faith called free will, we get to choose what we will do, say, read, watch, or listen to. Sometimes we choose the right things, but sadly we can also choose the wrong things that will eventually, if not immediately, lead us down the wrong path. Unfortunately, I could lump myself into that category of wrong choosers for much of my life.

God's Word never fails. *"For the word of God will never fail."* **Luke 1:37 (NLT)** One of the things I recommend that has helped me is a bible reading plan. Oftentimes these plans help you to read the entire Bible in one year. Simply search *'Bible reading plan'* online and you will receive tons of options. I really love reading the bible for so many reasons. One reason is it fills my mind with good things. *"Finally, brethren, whatever is true, whatever is honorable, whatever is* *right, whatever is pure, whatever is [a]lovely, whatever is of good repute, if there is any excellence and if anything worthy of praise, [b]dwell on these things."* **Philippians 4:8** Our minds can go astray pretty quickly. If I am filling my mind with God's Word, there is no room left for that to happen. Plus, this allows me to learn and experience the heart of God, which is immeasurable.

Prayer, worship, and God's Word have really been the tools that the Lord has used to help me get over during this final recovery process. My prayer is that I continue to walk this out each day. Soon I will walk into the newness of life where I am recovered, walking, and no longer bound to a wheelchair. Most importantly I desire to care for my family, who I love so much, and serve the Lord in what I believe to be the fullness of what He has called me to. Yes, recovery has been the most difficult part of becoming an amputee, but by prayer, worship, and God's Word I am getting over the most difficult part! *"These things I have spoken to you so that in Me you may have peace. In the world you have tribulation but take courage; I have overcome the world. "***John 16:33**

THE DAVIS FAMILY

CHILDREN (ZOE, MICHAEL, QJ) & ME

GRANDDAUGHTER (MIRACLE), DAUGHTER (ZOE), & ME

MOM (MARIAN) & SON (MILES)

Sarah - My Perfect Little Angel
Elena's Story

"I will give thanks to You, because I am awesomely and wonderfully made; Wonderful are Your works." Psalms 139:14 On August 14, 1986 - I gave birth to my precious little angel, my second daughter Sarah. Sarah was born with anencephaly. She was perfect in every way, except for what she did not have. Two minutes after she was born, she died. She will always be in my heart and in my mind. I always wonder what she would have been like, if she would have been anything like my precious Jessica or totally different. (They were full sisters). Would she have been like me? Looked like me?

When I found out that I was pregnant, we were living in Fairbanks, Alaska. My ex-husband was still in the Army, stationed at Fort Wainwright. It was a normal pregnancy. I was very healthy. I took care of myself, took my vitamins and iron daily. During my first few doctor appointments, everything was normal. Being an Army Veteran and an Army wife, I went to the Army hospital on Fort Wainwright for all of my care.

At six months pregnant, my stomach was huge. Since twins run in my family, the doctor decided to do an ultrasound to see if I was carrying twins. My ex-husband came with me to my appointment. When they did the first ultrasound, they were unable to get a clear image of the baby's head. I remember that I was wearing a long dress; they did not even have me change into a hospital gown. Next thing I know, several doctors, nurses, and med students were all in the room. Everyone was talking; however, no one was telling us anything. I was very upset, and they kept telling me to calm down. Then I became angry. Every time another person would come into the room, they would do another ultrasound. Then they brought in an x-ray machine. The baby's head was in the birth canal, so they manually tried to push her head up by doing an internal exam, and that made me even more angry. Finally, they were able to get a clear image of my baby. Everyone became silent.

Next, we met in the doctor's office.

I will never forget what he said, *"Some babies are born with deformities compatible with life, some babies are born with deformities incompatible with life. I am sorry to tell you, your baby has a deformity incompatible with life - Anencephaly."*

He handed us a medical book and proceeded to explain to us that when she was formed in my womb, she was formed without a brain. They did not have any answers as to why this happened.

Since this was a military hospital, and the doctor was a military doctor, he said, *"My advice to you is to go downtown and have an abortion. We are unable to do that here, and if you repeat this to anyone, I will deny it."*

At that time, they were not allowed to even advise a pregnant woman to terminate her pregnancy. It was not an option. To my ex-husband and me, abortion was murder. So, I became very angry. Defiantly, I told the doctors that they were not the final authority in this – ELOHIM is.

My baby will be born perfect and healthy.

And I walked out of the hospital. I was shaking. That night I cried, and I prayed, and Elohim assured me that my baby would be perfect. He promised me. And He keeps His promises. ***"Do not fear, for I am with you; Do not be afraid, for I am your God. I will strengthen you; I will also help you; I will also uphold you with My righteous right hand."*** **Isaiah 41:10**

I called my parents in New York. I wanted to go home. I wanted to be with my family, and have this baby at the same hospital, with the same doctor, where I gave birth to our daughter. Within a couple of weeks, my ex-husband got a compassionate reassignment to a recruiting battalion in upstate New York. We packed up our car, gave away some, and shipped the rest of our belongings to New York. We drove from Fairbanks to Germantown, New York. Eight days in the car – I was seven months pregnant, and our daughter was a year and a half old. My ex-husband drove pretty much the entire trip. We made the best of it. Our daughter ate French fries.

In New York, we stayed with my parents. They were overjoyed to finally have some time with their only grandchild, and I was able to rest. When we went for my first appointment with my doctor, he also did an ultrasound with the same results. We did not know what the baby's gender would be. My doctor said that from his experience, anencephalic babies are usually girls. Surprisingly, her heartbeat was strong. He was very realistic about what we were facing, but he respected my faith. I held on to my faith for dear life. ***"Consider it all joy, my brothers and sisters, when you encounter various trials, knowing that the testing of your faith produces endurance. And let endurance have its perfect result, so that you may be perfect and complete, lacking in nothing." James 1:2-4***

As my pregnancy continued to progress, I can remember her kicking inside me. I felt her movements, albeit she was not as energetic as my first baby. Listening to her heartbeat was wonderful. Everyone thought I was crazy. I wanted to buy stuff for her. I held on to Elohim's word. He told me that she would be perfect, period. It did not matter what anyone else thought.

On that Thursday morning, August 14, 1986, I arrived at the hospital, and they induced my labor. I was a month overdue. For nine hours I went through hard labor and still held on to my faith and the word Elohim had given me. I wanted pizza. I had an overwhelming sense of peace in the midst of it all. In the delivery room with us, was my aunt, who was a registered nurse. My mother decided not to stay in the room to witness the birth, so she and my other aunt were watching from the window. My father, one of my brothers, and other family members were outside the room with Jessica, who was then only 20 months old.

Then as it got closer to the time – her feet came out first. My aunt closed the blinds on the window. It was at that very moment I knew that she really was anencephalic. I remember becoming very serious and silent after that. Then finally at 6 PM – she was born. Our daughter, 6 pounds, 12 ounces, 18 inches long. The doctor immediately put a cap on her head, so I wouldn't see. They wrapped her up and put her in my arms. I unwrapped her and looked at her – she was absolutely perfect, except for what was missing. I did not look under the cap. Her face was the image of Jessica, but I also saw myself in her. I kissed her, and she opened her eyes and looked at me and smiled – as if to say, *"I love you Mommy – I will see you again in Heaven."* I told her I loved her, then I handed her to her father. They had just cut the umbilical cord. I literally saw the moment that her soul left her body, as she was in her father's arms at 6:02 PM. The 10 months inside the womb and 2 minutes outside the womb made a lifetime impact on me. I knew at that moment that she was absolutely perfect. Yes, she was, her little body was perfect, except for what was missing – she was – perfection in the presence of Yahweh!! Our earthly bodies are imperfect, but our heavenly bodies are pure, holy, and perfect. He promised me she would be perfect, and He does not lie. I still see her perfect little face, her perfect little body, and her perfect little hands, and feet. I see her eyes of perfect love looking up at me, and my tears falling on her face. ***"Who, by exerting that power which enables Him even to subject everything to Himself, will [not only] transform [but completely refashion] our earthly bodies so that they will be like His glorious, resurrected body."*** **Philippians 3:21 (AMP)**

I held her in my arms for about twenty minutes before they came to take her away. I wanted to take photos of her. My family took away the camera so I could not. I did not care that she was already gone, I wanted a photo of her to hold on to. That was a different time.

My doctor brought me a bottle of wine, and the nurses all ordered pizza for me. My uncle even brought me pizza. He was also our pastor. He stayed with us after visiting hours. I am crying as I am remembering. No one really knew what to do for me. I refused sedatives. I refused to break down in the hospital. I wanted to go home. I wanted to hold my other daughter and never let her go. ***"Even though I walk through the valley of the shadow of death, I fear no evil, for You are with me; Your rod and Your staff, they comfort me."* Psalms 23:4**

That night, I kept walking the floor of the birthing center. With tears falling down my face, I listened to the other mothers and their babies. My body was tired, but my mind kept me moving. Then my brother Joseph, who was not there during the birth, finally came to see me. The nurses graciously let him in long after visiting hours. He held me, and we both cried. Little did I know that just two months later, a fatal car accident would end his life here on earth.

We seek answers from Elohim; we don't always get the answers in the way that we want them. We don't always understand why things happen the way they do. We don't have to. He is Elohim. He promised that He would never leave us or forsake us. This life was never promised that it would be easy, but if we hold on to Him, it will be oh so worth it in the end.

Once we are born, it is with certainty that we will die. Sarah's life outside the womb was only two minutes. My faith was tried, and through it all my faith was strengthened. I held on to my faith no matter what. And it was that faith that kept me.

That was a rough year. Two months and one day later, my brother Joseph died at the age of 21... and not long after my marriage also died. (Three deaths in one year). I don't remember how strong I stood through those months – but I remember Who was with me and Who held me through it all. Those were the months He carried me. ***"And the LORD is the one who is going ahead of you; He will be with you. He will not desert you or abandon you. Do not fear and do not be dismayed."*** **Deuteronomy 31:8**

Over 20 years later, I was at the very same hospital visiting someone that was having a baby. Her nurse took one look at me and approached me. She told me how she remembered me and my daughter; – she was there when I gave birth to her. She said she could never forget the strength of my faith, and how I forced myself to get up after I gave birth and walk down the hall and spoke to her and others. The birthing center was full, and I was the only one without a baby to hold. And I was the only one with the strength to get up and keep pressing on. She even remembered that my brother, Joseph, showed up long after visiting hours and stayed with me for a while. I still can see him as he stood in the dimmed light of my room, as my ex-husband slept on the chair. That night, Joseph told me how much he loved me, and he promised that he would spend more time with me and with Jessica. He would never get to keep that promise. The nurse said she always wondered what happened to me. My faith made an impact on her life. And she hoped to one day tell me. And she did. Glory to Elohim!!!

My ex-husband and I were told that we may never be able to have another child born without defects. He already had a son from his first wife, and we already had our daughter, Jessica. After we divorced, I was blessed with my perfectly healthy son, Dominic, and he was blessed with another daughter, and another son. Glory to Elohim!!! Man does not understand it, and cannot fathom it, but Elohim!!

I truly thank Elohim for blessing me with Sarah for even just the moments that she was here. It was one of the hardest things I had to face in my life. No parent should ever have to bury their infant. Through it all I have seen the glory of Elohim and His perfect and unfailing love for me. And I know that one day, I will see her, as we both are in the presence of Yahweh!!!

I may not have any photos of you - but your image is in my mind and heart forever. . .

Sarah Padilla ~ Born and Died ~ 14 August 1986

As promised, she was perfect.
"I will always love you, my angel. See you in eternity!
Love and kisses and hugs, Mama."

Appendix A
Biblical Insights to Overcoming

Your Mouth	*Don't be silent, but be careful what you speak*
Your Eyes	*Be careful what you allow into your eye gate*
Your Ears	*Listen only to wise counsel*
Your Worship	*Praise & worship must be a way of life*
Your Sword	*Don't neglect the Word*
Your Surroundings	*Surround yourself with positive people only*
Your Losses	*Get rid of the negativity*
Your Mind	*Think on good things*
Your Computer Program – Overcome 2.0	*Upload faith & Download fear*

Appendix B
Scriptures

Old Testament Scriptures

~Pentateuch~

Deuteronomy 31:8
"And the LORD is the one who is going ahead of you; He will be with you. He will not desert you or abandon you. Do not fear and do not be dismayed."

~Historical Books~

2 Chronicles 20:22
"When they began singing and praising, the Lord set ambushes against the sons of Ammon, Moab, and Mount Seir, who had come against Judah; so, they were [a]routed."

~Poetic Books~

Proverbs 3:5-6
"Trust in the Lord with all your heart And do not lean on your own understanding. In all your ways acknowledge Him, And He will make your paths straight."

Proverbs 4:12
"There is a way which seems right to a man, But its end is the way of death."

Psalms 23:4
"Even though I walk through the valley of the shadow of death, I fear no evil, for You are with me; Your rod and Your staff, they comfort me."

Psalm 91:4-7

"You will not be afraid of the terror by night, Or of the arrow that flies by day; Of the pestilence that [a]stalks in darkness, Or of the destruction that lays waste at noon. A thousand may fall at your side And ten thousand at your right hand, But it shall not approach you."

Psalm 118:24
"This is the day that the Lord has made; Let us rejoice and be glad in it!"

Psalms 139:14
"I will give thanks to You, because I am awesomely and wonderfully made; Wonderful are Your works. . ."

Psalm 141:3
"Set a guard, O Lord, [a]over my mouth; Keep watch over the door of my lips. Do not incline my heart to any evil thing, To practice deeds [a]of wickedness."

~Prophetic Books (Major Prophets) ~

Isaiah 41:10
"Do not fear, for I am with you; Do not be afraid, for I am your God. I will strengthen you; I will also help you, I will also uphold you with My righteous right hand."

Isaiah 54:17a (NIV)
"No weapon formed against you shall prosper"

Jeremiah 33:3

"Call to Me and I will answer you, and I will tell you great and mighty things, which you do not know.'

New Testament Scriptures

~Gospels~

John 16:33
"These things I have spoken to you so that in Me you may have peace. In the world you have tribulation but take courage; I have overcome the world."

~Pauline Epistles~

Romans 5:3-5
"And not only this, but [c]we also exult in our tribulations, knowing that tribulation brings about perseverance; 4 and perseverance, proven character; and proven character, hope; 5 and hope does not disappoint, because the love of God has been poured out within our hearts through the Holy Spirit who was given to us."

Romans 8:37 (NIV)
"No, in all these things we are more than conquerors through him who loved us."

1 Corinthians 15:57
".... but thanks be to God, who gives us the victory through our Lord Jesus Christ."

Philippians 3:13b
"…. forgetting what lies behind and reaching forward to what lies ahead,"

Philippians 3:21 (AMP)
"Who, by exerting that power which enables Him even to subject everything to Himself, will [not only] transform [but completely refashion] our earthly bodies so that they will be like His glorious, resurrected body."

Philippians 4:6-7
" Be anxious for nothing, but in everything by prayer and supplication with thanksgiving let your requests be made known to God. 7 And the peace of God, which surpasses all [a]comprehension, will guard your hearts and your minds in Christ Jesus."

Philippians 4:8
"Finally, brethren, whatever is true, whatever is honorable, whatever is right, whatever is pure, whatever is [a]lovely, whatever is of good repute, if there is any excellence and if anything worthy of praise, [b]dwell on these things."

1 Thessalonians 5:17
"Pray without ceasing"

2 Timothy 1:7 (NKJV)
" For God has not given us a spirit of fear, but of power and of love and of a sound mind."

2 Timothy 3:16

"All Scripture is [a]inspired by God and profitable for teaching, for reproof, for correction, for [b]training in righteousness;"

~General Epistles~

Hebrews 4:12 (NKJV)
"For the word of God is living and powerful, and sharper than any two-edged sword, piercing even to the division of soul and spirit, and of joints and marrow, and is a discerner of the thoughts and intents of the heart."

James 1:2-4
"Consider it all joy, my brothers and sisters, when you encounter various trials, knowing that the testing of your faith produces endurance. And let endurance have its perfect result, so that you may be perfect and complete, lacking in nothing."

James 1:5
"But if any of you lacks wisdom, let him ask of God, who gives to all generously and [a]without reproach, and it will be given to him."

1 Peter 5:8b
"Your adversary, the devil, prowls around like a roaring lion, seeking someone to devour."

1 John 1:9
"If we confess our sins, He is faithful and righteous to forgive us our sins and to cleanse us from all unrighteousness.

1 John 5:5
"Who is the one who overcomes the world, but the one who believes that Jesus is the Son of God"?

Appendix C
About the Co-Authors

Scotti Taylor

Scotti lives with her husband and four teenaged children in sunny North County San Diego, California. She owns and operates a successful balloon business, while spending most of her time managing schedules and driving her crew. Scotti enjoys life as a busy, Jesus-loving woman who loves her family and friends. Her life verse is" **You will not be afraid of the terror by night, Or of the arrow that flies by day;"** **Psalm 91:5.**

Lakesha Davis

*Lakesha's life verse is **"Be strong and courageous, do not be afraid or in dread of them, for the Lord your God is the One who is going with you. He will not desert you or abandon you."** Deuteronomy 31:6 She works with mental health adolescent girls, and one day wishes to own her own funeral home. She has three children and six grandchildren whom she loves dearly. Lakesha loves God, spending time on the beach, going to church, and playing with her grandbabies, who are her pride and joy. She currently resides in Houston, TX.*

LaTroy Broadnax

*LaTroy works in sales. His hobbies include playing dominos with his wife and enjoying the outdoors. He is also a singer and songwriter in his spare time. LaTroy has one daughter and resides in Houston, TX with his wife. His life verse is **"For God so loved the world, that He gave His only Son, so that everyone who believes in Him will not perish, but have eternal life."** John 3:16*

Elena Leno

Elena's life verse is **"He did not hesitate about the promise of Elohim through unbelief, but was strengthened in belief, giving esteem to Elohim, and being completely persuaded that, what He had promised, He was also able to do."** *Romans 4:20-21 (TS2009) She is a US Army Veteran, a real estate professional, property manager, and notary public in the state of Florida. Elena is the mother of three and grandmother of four. In her spare time, she enjoys walking the beautiful beaches of Florida, where she resides, and nature photography.*

Appendix D
About the Anthologist

Tamatha A. Davis

*Tamatha's life verse is **"Not unto us O Lord, not unto us, but to your name be the glory for your love and faithfulness." Psalm 115:1 (NIV)** A pastor's wife, homeschool mother of four amazing children (three have graduated), and speaker added published author to her list of accomplishments in 2014! The book **40 Days to Freedom: A Woman's Daily Devotional** is just a sampling of the devotional e-mails that she began sending to her friends and co-workers after returning from her first mission's trip to Africa in 1999.*

In 2003, Tamatha A. Davis left her corporate position in the legal department of a major computer company to stay home with her newly adopted three boys ages two, three, and seven. Her husband had been recently laid off from a major telecommunications company. In just six months Tamatha and her husband Michael went from "DINKS" (Double Income – No Kids) to three kids with no income! Out of necessity, Holy Smokes BBQ & Catering was born in 2004.

Two years later not only was she a business owner and a stay-at-home mother, but a homeschooling mother as well. Eventually, she found Classical Conversations, a Christian classical homeschooling organization that provided the tools she needed to stay the course in homeschooling her growing family. The Davis' adopted a little girl in 2009.

Tamatha spent a decade working for Classical Conversations in various roles. As a State Manager she opened over thirty new homeschooling communities in and around the Houston area. Her last position was in Communications and Public Relations. She is still homeschooling her one daughter that has not yet graduated, and still married to the love of her life for almost 27 years.

In 2011, the Davis family moved to Houston to plant Christ's Peace Family Worship Center. Tamatha and her husband Michael A.E. Davis currently serve at North Mount Olive Church where he is the pastor.

In 2018, Tamatha became an amputee losing her right leg in an above the knee amputation due to Peripheral Arterial Disease (PAD), a rare vascular disorder. However, she has not let that stop her. She continues her pursuit to encourage women that no matter what you go through you can still have joy in the midst of the journey. Her book **Joyous Journey of Loss** was published in August 2019, and she launched JJ Retreat & Conference the same year. She plans to host a yearly conference encouraging women from all walks of life to live free, transparent, and purposeful lives.

How I Got Over: Stories of Faith and Courage in the Face of Adversity is her fourth book and second anthology. She has also published several books through the publishing company that she owns – Sivad Publishing. As a pastor's wife, mother, grandmother, author, entrepreneur, book coach, publisher, and speaker Tamatha is passionate about seeing the cup "half full" instead of "half empty," discipleship, and her family. Tamatha lives in Houston, TX. with her husband and children. She has one beautiful granddaughter – Miracle.

If you are interested in publishing your story, contact Tamatha:
(davis.tamatha@gmail.com) or
Sivad Publishing (www.tamathadavis.com)

She is currently interviewing authors for her next anthology.

www.ingramcontent.com/pod-product-compliance
Lightning Source LLC
Chambersburg PA
CBHW071446030726
47593CB00003B/909